BRAVE NEW ECONOMY

Understanding Cryptocurrencies

Geoffrey Zachary

CONTENTS

commerce

Brave New Economy:
Understanding Cryptocurrencies

PART I:
INTRODUCTION TO CRYPTOCURRENCIES

CHAPTER 1: THE EVOLUTION OF MONEY

Introduction:
Money is a fundamental concept that has played a pivotal role in shaping human civilization. Throughout history, various forms of money have emerged, reflecting the economic, social, and technological advancements of different eras. This chapter explores the fascinating journey of money's evolution, from its earliest origins to the modern era of cryptocurrencies.

The Barter System:
Before the concept of money existed, societies relied on a barter system for trade. Individuals exchanged goods and services directly, based on their needs and the availability of desired items. While this system worked to some extent, it had inherent limitations, such as the need for a double coincidence of wants and difficulties in determining fair exchange rates.

The Birth of Currency:
As societies grew more complex, the need for a more standardized medium of exchange arose. The introduction of commodity money marked a significant milestone in the evolution of money. Items with intrinsic value, such as shells, beads, or precious metals, were used as a widely accepted form of payment. Examples include cowrie shells in ancient China, gold coins in ancient Rome, and silver coins in medieval Europe.

The Rise of Paper Money:
With the expansion of trade and commerce, carrying large amounts of precious metal coins became cumbersome. To address this challenge, governments and financial institutions began issuing paper money backed by a reserve of gold or silver. This transition to paper currency allowed for easier transportation, storage, and standardized denominations. The establishment of the first central banks in the 17th century further enhanced the stability and credibility of paper money.

The Era of Fiat Money:
In the 20th century, the global financial system gradually moved away from the gold standard, and fiat money emerged as the dominant form of currency. Fiat money is not backed by a physical commodity but derives its value from government regulation and the trust and confidence placed in the issuing authority. This shift provided governments with more flexibility in managing their economies but also introduced challenges related to inflation and economic stability.

The Digital Revolution and Electronic Payments:
The advent of computers and the internet propelled the next phase in the evolution of money. Electronic payment systems, such as credit cards, debit cards, and online banking, revolutionized the way we conduct financial transactions. These systems enable instantaneous transfers, enhance convenience, and reduce reliance on physical currency.

Cryptocurrencies: A Paradigm Shift in Money:
In recent years, the rise of cryptocurrencies, such as Bitcoin, Ethereum, and others, has disrupted traditional notions of money. Built on blockchain technology, cryptocurrencies offer decentralized and secure peer-to-peer transactions, eliminating the need for intermediaries. They also introduce the concept of digital scarcity and enable programmable money through smart contracts. Bitcoin, introduced in 2009, paved the way for this new

era of cryptocurrencies.

Real-Life Examples:
Bitcoin, the first and most well-known cryptocurrency, has had a profound impact on the financial landscape. Its decentralized nature allows for censorship-resistant transactions, making it particularly valuable in countries with unstable governments or limited access to traditional banking services. For example, in Venezuela, citizens have turned to Bitcoin as a store of value and a means to bypass currency controls and hyperinflation.

Another real-life example is the growth of blockchain-based payment systems. Ripple, a cryptocurrency platform, has partnered with financial institutions worldwide to facilitate fast and low-cost cross-border transactions. This technology has the potential to revolutionize international remittances and improve financial inclusion for the unbanked.

Conclusion:
The evolution of money has been a continuous journey, driven by the need for more efficient, secure, and accessible means of exchange. From bartering to cryptocurrencies, each stage has brought new opportunities and challenges. Cryptocurrencies represent a paradigm shift in how we think about money, offering unique features and possibilities for the future of finance. As we navigate this rapidly changing landscape, understanding the evolution of money provides valuable insights into the potential impact of cryptocurrencies and the brave new economy that lies ahead.

CHAPTER 2: WHAT ARE CRYPTOCURRENCIES?

Introduction:
Cryptocurrencies have gained significant attention and popularity in recent years, revolutionizing the way we perceive and use money. This chapter explores the concept of cryptocurrencies, delving into their characteristics, underlying technology, and the potential they hold for reshaping the financial landscape.

Defining Cryptocurrencies:
Cryptocurrencies are digital or virtual currencies that utilize cryptography for secure transactions, control the creation of new units, and operate independently of a central bank. They are decentralized, meaning they operate on a peer-to-peer network without the need for intermediaries like banks. Cryptocurrencies derive their value from the principles of supply and demand, as well as the utility they provide within their respective ecosystems.

Blockchain Technology:
At the heart of cryptocurrencies lies blockchain technology, a distributed ledger system that records and verifies transactions across multiple computers or nodes. The blockchain ensures transparency, security, and immutability of the transaction history. It is through the blockchain that cryptocurrencies achieve their decentralization and enable secure peer-to-peer transactions.

Key Characteristics of Cryptocurrencies:

1. Decentralization: Cryptocurrencies operate on decentralized networks, removing the need for a central authority and enabling individuals to have direct control over their digital assets.

2. Security: Cryptocurrencies use cryptographic techniques to secure transactions and control the creation of new units. This enhances the integrity and privacy of the financial transactions.

3. Transparency: The transaction history of cryptocurrencies is recorded on the blockchain, which is accessible to all network participants. This transparency ensures accountability and reduces the risk of fraud.

4. Limited Supply: Many cryptocurrencies have a limited supply, meaning there is a cap on the total number of units that can ever be created. This scarcity can contribute to their value and potential as a store of wealth.

Real-Life Examples:

Bitcoin: Bitcoin is the first and most well-known cryptocurrency, introduced in 2009. It operates on the principles of decentralization and uses the proof-of-work consensus mechanism to secure transactions. Bitcoin has gained global recognition and acceptance, with numerous merchants and businesses now accepting it as a form of payment. It has also experienced significant price volatility, attracting investors and speculators.

Ethereum: Ethereum is a cryptocurrency and a decentralized platform that enables the development of smart contracts and decentralized applications (DApps). It introduced the concept of programmable money, allowing developers to create and deploy applications on its blockchain. Ethereum's native currency, Ether, is used to power these applications and execute smart contracts. This programmability has opened a wide range of possibilities for innovation and decentralized finance.

Discussion:

Cryptocurrencies have generated excitement and debate due to their disruptive potential in the financial industry. Advocates argue that cryptocurrencies can provide financial inclusion, security, and privacy, particularly for individuals in underserved regions or those facing economic instability. They also highlight the potential for faster and cheaper cross-border transactions, removing the need for intermediaries like banks.

However, there are also concerns and challenges associated with cryptocurrencies. Price volatility, regulatory uncertainties, and the potential for illicit activities have raised questions about their long-term stability and adoption. Additionally, the energy consumption associated with certain cryptocurrencies, such as Bitcoin, has drawn attention to the environmental impact of their mining processes.

Conclusion:
Cryptocurrencies represent a significant advancement in the way we perceive and use money. Built on blockchain technology, they offer decentralized, secure, and transparent transactions. Bitcoin and Ethereum are prime examples of cryptocurrencies that have reshaped the financial landscape and sparked a wave of innovation. As the world embraces this digital revolution, understanding the characteristics and potential of cryptocurrencies becomes essential for individuals, businesses, and policymakers. This chapter provides a foundational understanding of what cryptocurrencies are, their underlying technology, and their implications for the future of finance.

CHAPTER 3: THE BLOCKCHAIN TECHNOLOGY BEHIND CRYPTOCURRENCIES

Introduction:
Blockchain technology serves as the backbone of cryptocurrencies, enabling secure and transparent transactions. In this chapter, we delve into the intricacies of blockchain technology, its fundamental principles, and its role in revolutionizing the financial landscape.

Understanding Blockchain Technology:
At its core, a blockchain is a decentralized, distributed ledger that records and verifies transactions across multiple nodes or computers. It operates on a consensus mechanism, ensuring agreement on the validity of transactions without the need for a central authority. The blockchain is structured as a chain of blocks, with each block containing a set of transactions. These blocks are linked together using cryptographic hash functions, forming an immutable record of all transactions.

Key Components of Blockchain Technology:
1. Decentralization: The decentralized nature of blockchain eliminates the need for a central authority, such as a bank or government, to validate and authorize transactions. Instead, transactions are verified by a network of participants known as

nodes, ensuring transparency, and reducing the risk of fraud.

2. Consensus Mechanisms: Consensus mechanisms are the algorithms used to achieve agreement among nodes on the validity of transactions. Examples include Proof of Work (PoW), Proof of Stake (PoS), and Delegated Proof of Stake (DPoS). These mechanisms incentivize participants to act honestly and maintain the security of the blockchain.

3. Cryptographic Security: Blockchain technology employs cryptographic techniques to secure transactions and maintain the integrity of the data. Each transaction is digitally signed using public-key cryptography, ensuring that only the authorized participants can access and modify the information.

Real-Life Examples:

Bitcoin: The Bitcoin blockchain is the first and most well-known implementation of blockchain technology. It operates on a PoW consensus mechanism, where miners compete to solve complex mathematical puzzles to validate transactions and add them to the blockchain. Bitcoin's blockchain has proven to be secure and resistant to tampering, providing a robust foundation for the digital currency.

Ethereum: Ethereum introduced the concept of smart contracts, which are self-executing agreements stored on the blockchain. The Ethereum blockchain supports the execution of these smart contracts, enabling the development of decentralized applications (DApps) and the creation of new cryptocurrencies (tokens) on its platform. Ethereum's blockchain has paved the way for innovative use cases beyond simple financial transactions.

Discussion:
Blockchain technology has the potential to revolutionize various industries beyond cryptocurrencies. Its decentralized and transparent nature makes it suitable for applications such as supply chain management, healthcare records, voting systems,

and more. By providing an immutable and auditable record, blockchain technology enhances trust and eliminates the need for intermediaries in many processes.

While blockchain offers numerous benefits, it also faces challenges. Scalability remains a concern, as the transaction processing capacity of some blockchains is limited. Additionally, energy consumption associated with certain consensus mechanisms, particularly PoW, has raised environmental concerns. Ongoing research and development are focused on addressing these challenges and exploring alternative consensus mechanisms to improve efficiency and sustainability.

Conclusion:
Blockchain technology serves as the underlying infrastructure for cryptocurrencies, offering decentralized and secure transactions. Bitcoin and Ethereum are prime examples of blockchain implementations that have transformed the financial landscape and paved the way for innovative applications. Understanding the fundamental principles and components of blockchain technology is essential for individuals and businesses looking to leverage its potential. This chapter provides an overview of blockchain technology, its decentralized nature, consensus mechanisms, and cryptographic security. With its potential to revolutionize various industries, blockchain is poised to reshape the way we conduct transactions and establish trust in the digital age.

CHAPTER 4: THE ADVANTAGES AND DISADVANTAGES OF CRYPTOCURRENCIES

Introduction:
Cryptocurrencies have gained significant attention in recent years as an alternative form of digital currency. In this chapter, we explore the advantages and disadvantages of cryptocurrencies, highlighting their potential benefits and the challenges they present in various aspects of finance and commerce.

Advantages of Cryptocurrencies:

1. Decentralization: One of the key advantages of cryptocurrencies is their decentralized nature. They operate on a peer-to-peer network, eliminating the need for intermediaries such as banks. This decentralized structure provides greater control and autonomy over one's financial transactions.

2. Security: Cryptocurrencies employ advanced cryptographic techniques to secure transactions. The use of cryptographic hash functions and digital signatures ensures the integrity and confidentiality of the transactions, reducing the risk of fraud and hacking.

3. Transparency: Blockchain, the underlying technology of most cryptocurrencies, offers transparent and immutable records of

transactions. This transparency helps to prevent fraud and promotes trust among participants, as anyone can verify the transaction history on the blockchain.

4. Accessibility: Cryptocurrencies enable financial inclusion by providing access to financial services for individuals who are unbanked or underbanked. With just an internet connection, anyone can participate in cryptocurrency transactions, regardless of their geographical location.

5. Speed and Efficiency: Cryptocurrency transactions can be executed quickly, particularly for cross-border transactions. Traditional banking systems often involve intermediaries and lengthy processing times, whereas cryptocurrencies enable near-instantaneous transfers.

Disadvantages of Cryptocurrencies:

1. Volatility: Cryptocurrencies are known for their price volatility. The value of cryptocurrencies can fluctuate significantly within short periods, posing risks for investors and merchants who accept cryptocurrencies as a form of payment. This volatility can limit their mainstream adoption as a stable medium of exchange.

2. Regulatory Challenges: The decentralized nature of cryptocurrencies poses challenges for regulatory bodies. The absence of a central authority makes it difficult to enforce regulations, combat illegal activities, and protect consumers. Governments worldwide are grappling with the development of suitable regulatory frameworks to address these concerns.

3. Scalability: Scalability remains a challenge for many cryptocurrencies. As the number of transactions increases, some blockchain networks experience congestion, leading to delays and increased transaction fees. This scalability issue needs to be addressed for cryptocurrencies to become widely adopted as a mainstream payment method.

4. Energy Consumption: The mining process, particularly in

Proof of Work (PoW) cryptocurrencies, consumes a significant amount of energy. This has raised environmental concerns as cryptocurrencies gain popularity. However, alternative consensus mechanisms such as Proof of Stake (PoS) and delegated PoS are being developed to address these energy consumption issues.

Real-Life Examples:

Bitcoin: Bitcoin, the first and most well-known cryptocurrency, has demonstrated both the advantages and disadvantages of cryptocurrencies. It offers decentralized transactions, security, and accessibility, but also faces challenges such as price volatility and scalability.

Stablecoins: Stablecoins are a type of cryptocurrency that is pegged to a stable asset like a fiat currency or a commodity. They aim to address the volatility issue by maintaining a stable value. Examples include Tether (USDT) and USD Coin (USDC), which provide stability for users seeking a reliable store of value.

Discussion:
The advantages and disadvantages of cryptocurrencies must be carefully considered as they continue to evolve and gain prominence. While cryptocurrencies offer decentralization, security, and accessibility, challenges such as price volatility, scalability, and regulatory concerns remain. Overcoming these challenges is essential for cryptocurrencies to achieve widespread adoption and integration into the global financial system.

Conclusion:
Cryptocurrencies offer unique advantages and disadvantages in the realm of finance and commerce. Their decentralized nature, security, and accessibility present opportunities for financial inclusion and innovation. However, challenges related to volatility, scalability, and regulatory frameworks must be addressed to ensure their long-term viability. As cryptocurrencies continue to evolve, striking a balance between harnessing their advantages and mitigating their disadvantages is crucial for their

successful integration into the global economy.

PART II: KEY CONCEPTS IN CRYPTOCURRENCIES

CHAPTER 5: CRYPTOCURRENCY MINING AND PROOF-OF-WORK

Introduction:
Cryptocurrency mining plays a pivotal role in the operation and security of blockchain networks. In this chapter, we delve into the process of cryptocurrency mining, focusing on the widely used consensus mechanism called Proof-of-Work (PoW). We explore the intricacies of mining, its purpose, and its impact on the cryptocurrency ecosystem.

Understanding Cryptocurrency Mining:
Cryptocurrency mining involves validating and adding new transactions to the blockchain ledger. Miners utilize computational power to solve complex mathematical puzzles that secure the network and maintain the integrity of the blockchain. Successful miners are rewarded with newly minted coins as an incentive for their participation in the network.

Proof-of-Work (PoW) Consensus:
Proof-of-Work is a consensus mechanism used in many cryptocurrencies, including Bitcoin and Ethereum. It ensures that the network reaches a consensus on the validity of transactions and prevents double-spending. PoW requires miners to compete by solving mathematical puzzles, known as hashes, in a race

to find the correct solution. The first miner to solve the puzzle and validate the block of transactions is rewarded with cryptocurrency.

The Mining Process:
1. Hashing: Miners use powerful hardware and specialized software to perform numerous calculations, known as hashing, to find a hash that meets specific criteria. The hashing process involves taking an input and generating a fixed-size output unique to that input.

2. Difficulty Adjustment: The difficulty of the cryptographic puzzle adjusts dynamically to ensure that new blocks are added to the blockchain at a predefined rate. This adjustment ensures that mining remains challenging, irrespective of the computational power available.

3. Block Validation: Once a miner successfully finds the correct hash, they broadcast it to the network. Other nodes in the network then verify the solution and validate the block of transactions. If the block is deemed valid, it is added to the blockchain.

Energy Consumption and Environmental Impact:
Cryptocurrency mining, particularly in PoW-based cryptocurrencies, has been criticized for its high energy consumption. The computational power required for mining and the competition among miners results in significant electricity consumption. Bitcoin mining, for example, consumes a substantial amount of energy, comparable to the energy consumption of some countries. This has raised concerns about its environmental impact and carbon footprint.

Real-Life Examples:
1. Bitcoin Mining: Bitcoin mining is the most well-known example of cryptocurrency mining. Miners compete globally to solve cryptographic puzzles and earn Bitcoin rewards. The mining process has evolved, from individuals using regular CPUs

to specialized mining hardware known as ASICs (Application-Specific Integrated Circuits).

2. Ethereum Mining: Ethereum, the second-largest cryptocurrency by market capitalization, also relies on PoW mining. However, Ethereum has announced plans to transition to a more energy-efficient consensus mechanism called Proof-of-Stake (PoS). This transition aims to address the energy consumption concerns associated with mining.

Discussion:
Cryptocurrency mining, particularly in PoW-based cryptocurrencies, has contributed to the growth and security of blockchain networks. However, the energy consumption associated with mining raises environmental concerns. As the popularity of cryptocurrencies continues to increase, finding more energy-efficient consensus mechanisms, such as Proof-of-Stake, becomes crucial to mitigate the environmental impact.

Conclusion:
Cryptocurrency mining, powered by the Proof-of-Work consensus mechanism, serves as the backbone of many blockchain networks. It ensures the security and integrity of transactions while rewarding miners for their computational efforts. However, the energy consumption associated with mining raises environmental concerns. As the cryptocurrency ecosystem evolves, exploring more sustainable consensus mechanisms and energy-efficient mining practices will be vital to address these challenges and create a more sustainable future for cryptocurrencies.

CHAPTER 6: CRYPTOCURRENCY WALLETS AND SECURITY

Introduction:
In the world of cryptocurrencies, wallets play a crucial role in securely storing, managing, and transacting with digital assets. This chapter explores the concept of cryptocurrency wallets and the importance of security measures to protect users' funds. We will discuss different types of wallets, their features, and best practices for ensuring the safety of cryptocurrencies.

Types of Cryptocurrency Wallets:
1. Software Wallets: Software wallets are applications installed on electronic devices, such as computers or smartphones. They offer convenience and accessibility, allowing users to manage their cryptocurrencies through user-friendly interfaces. Examples include desktop wallets, mobile wallets, and online wallets.

2. Hardware Wallets: Hardware wallets are physical devices designed specifically for storing cryptocurrencies. They provide an extra layer of security by keeping private keys offline and away from potential online threats. Hardware wallets are highly secure and resistant to hacking attempts. Popular hardware wallets include Ledger, Trezor, and KeepKey.

3. Paper Wallets: Paper wallets involve printing private and public keys on paper. They offer an offline storage option, providing a high level of security as long as the physical document is kept safe from damage or loss. However, paper wallets can be vulnerable to theft if not properly secured.

4. Custodial Wallets: Custodial wallets are wallets provided by third-party service providers, such as exchanges or online platforms. These wallets store users' private keys on their behalf, allowing for easy access and management of cryptocurrencies. However, custodial wallets come with a higher risk of security breaches and rely on users' trust in the service provider.

Security Measures for Cryptocurrency Wallets:
1. Strong Passwords: Creating strong, unique passwords for wallets is essential. A combination of uppercase and lowercase letters, numbers, and special characters should be used.

2. Two-Factor Authentication (2FA): Enabling 2FA adds an extra layer of security by requiring users to provide a second form of verification, such as a code sent to their mobile device, in addition to their password.

3. Regular Software Updates: Keeping wallet software up to date ensures that users benefit from the latest security enhancements and bug fixes.

4. Cold Storage: Storing cryptocurrencies in offline wallets or hardware wallets, known as cold storage, provides enhanced security by keeping private keys offline and away from potential online threats.

5. Backup and Recovery: Creating regular backups of wallet data and securely storing them in multiple locations helps protect against data loss and allows for easy recovery in case of device failure or loss.

Real-Life Examples:

1. Mt. Gox Hack: Mt. Gox, once the largest Bitcoin exchange, experienced a major security breach in 2014, resulting in the loss of approximately 850,000 Bitcoins. This incident highlighted the importance of secure storage and prompted increased awareness about wallet security practices.

2. Ledger Data Breach: In 2020, Ledger, a popular hardware wallet manufacturer, suffered a data breach that exposed customer information, including email addresses and phone numbers. This event emphasized the significance of safeguarding personal information and the potential risks associated with custodial services.

Discussion:
As the adoption of cryptocurrencies grows, ensuring the security of cryptocurrency wallets becomes paramount. While advancements in wallet technology have made managing cryptocurrencies more convenient, they have also attracted malicious actors seeking to exploit vulnerabilities. Users must understand the different types of wallets available and adopt best practices for wallet security.

Conclusion:
Cryptocurrency wallets are integral to securely storing and managing digital assets. By selecting the right type of wallet and implementing security measures such as strong passwords, 2FA, regular software updates, and cold storage, users can minimize the risk of theft or loss of their cryptocurrencies. As the cryptocurrency ecosystem evolves, continuous education and awareness about wallet security practices are essential for individuals to safeguard their funds in the brave new economy of cryptocurrencies.

CHAPTER 7: CRYPTOCURRENCY EXCHANGES AND TRADING

Introduction:
Cryptocurrency exchanges play a pivotal role in the world of digital currencies, serving as platforms where users can buy, sell, and trade various cryptocurrencies. This chapter explores the intricacies of cryptocurrency exchanges, including their functions, types, and the risks and benefits associated with cryptocurrency trading.

Functions of Cryptocurrency Exchanges:
1. Marketplaces: Cryptocurrency exchanges act as online marketplaces where buyers and sellers can interact and trade cryptocurrencies. They provide a platform for users to place buy and sell orders, facilitating the exchange of digital assets.

2. Price Discovery: Exchanges help establish the value of cryptocurrencies through the forces of supply and demand. The prices of cryptocurrencies are determined by the transactions taking place on the exchange, reflecting the market sentiment and perceived value of the digital assets.

3. Wallet Services: Many exchanges provide wallet services, allowing users to store their cryptocurrencies directly on the

platform. However, it is important to note that storing funds on an exchange carries certain risks, as the control of the private keys lies with the exchange.

Types of Cryptocurrency Exchanges:
1. Centralized Exchanges: Centralized exchanges (CEX) are the most common type of cryptocurrency exchange. They are operated by a single entity and act as intermediaries between buyers and sellers. CEXs maintain order books, match buy and sell orders, and facilitate transactions. Examples of centralized exchanges include Binance, Coinbase, and Kraken.

2. Decentralized Exchanges: Decentralized exchanges (DEX) operate on blockchain technology and do not rely on a central authority to facilitate trade. DEXs allow users to trade directly with one another using smart contracts, providing greater control and privacy over their funds. Examples of decentralized exchanges include Uniswap, SushiSwap, and PancakeSwap.

Risks and Benefits of Cryptocurrency Trading:
1. Volatility: Cryptocurrency markets are known for their high volatility, with prices experiencing significant fluctuations within short periods. While this volatility presents profit opportunities, it also carries the risk of substantial losses.

2. Security Risks: Trading on centralized exchanges involves entrusting funds to third-party platforms, which can be vulnerable to hacking attempts and security breaches. Users must exercise caution and choose reputable and secure exchanges.

3. Liquidity: Liquidity refers to the ease of buying or selling a cryptocurrency without impacting its market price. Larger centralized exchanges generally offer higher liquidity, allowing for more efficient trading.

4. Accessibility: Cryptocurrency exchanges provide access to a wide range of digital assets, allowing users to diversify their investment portfolios and participate in the emerging

cryptocurrency market.

Real-Life Examples:
1. Mt. Gox Collapse: Mt. Gox, once the largest Bitcoin exchange, suffered a catastrophic hack in 2014, resulting in the loss of approximately 850,000 Bitcoins. This incident highlighted the importance of selecting reliable and secure exchanges and the need for proper security measures.

2. Binance Growth: Binance, founded in 2017, quickly emerged as one of the largest cryptocurrencies exchanges due to its user-friendly interface, a wide range of available cryptocurrencies, and robust security measures. It became a prominent player in the industry and continues to attract a significant user base.

Discussion:
Cryptocurrency exchanges serve as key gateways for individuals and institutions to enter the world of digital currencies. However, the risks associated with trading on exchanges, such as security vulnerabilities and market volatility, must be carefully considered. Users must conduct thorough research, choose reputable exchanges, and adopt appropriate security measures to protect their funds.

Conclusion:
Cryptocurrency exchanges enable users to participate in the exciting and evolving world of digital assets. Whether trading on centralized or decentralized exchanges, individuals need to understand the risks and benefits involved. By exercising caution, staying informed, and adopting proper security measures, individuals can navigate the cryptocurrency trading landscape with confidence. As the cryptocurrency market continues to mature, exchanges play a vital role in facilitating the growth and adoption of digital currencies.

CHAPTER 8: CRYPTOCURRENCY TOKENS AND SMART CONTRACTS

Introduction:
Cryptocurrency tokens and smart contracts are fundamental components of blockchain technology. This chapter explores the concept of cryptocurrency tokens, their types, and the role of smart contracts in enabling programmable and self-executing agreements on the blockchain.

Cryptocurrency Tokens:
1. Utility Tokens: Utility tokens are designed to provide access to a specific product or service within a blockchain ecosystem. They serve as a medium of exchange and represent the right to use or access certain functionalities. Examples include Ethereum's Ether (ETH), which is used to pay transaction fees and deploy smart contracts on the Ethereum network.

2. Security Tokens: Security tokens represent ownership in a real-world asset, such as shares in a company or fractional ownership of a property. These tokens are subject to securities regulations and provide investors with rights and entitlements, such as dividends or voting rights. Security tokens aim to bridge the gap between traditional financial markets and blockchain technology.

3. Stablecoins: Stablecoins are a type of cryptocurrency that aims to maintain a stable value by pegging it to a fiat currency or an underlying asset like gold. Stablecoins provide stability and can be used as a medium of exchange and store of value. Examples include Tether (USDT) and USD Coin (USDC), which are pegged to the value of the US dollar.

Smart Contracts:
Smart contracts are self-executing contracts with the terms of the agreement directly written into code on the blockchain. These contracts automatically execute and enforce the agreed-upon terms, removing the need for intermediaries. Smart contracts enable a wide range of applications, from financial transactions to supply chain management and decentralized applications (DApps).

Real-Life Examples:
1. Initial Coin Offerings (ICOs): ICOs were a popular fundraising method during the cryptocurrency boom of 2017. Companies would issue tokens to investors in exchange for funds to finance their projects. However, many ICOs lacked proper regulation, leading to fraudulent schemes and scams. This highlighted the importance of regulatory oversight and investor protection.

2. Decentralized Finance (DeFi): DeFi protocols, built on blockchain platforms like Ethereum, leverage smart contracts to offer traditional financial services, such as lending, borrowing, and trading, in a decentralized manner. Examples include decentralized exchanges like Uniswap and lending platforms like Aave. DeFi has gained significant traction and demonstrated the potential of smart contracts in revolutionizing traditional financial systems.

Discussion:
Cryptocurrency tokens and smart contracts have transformed the way we think about value exchange and agreements. They enable new economic models, decentralized governance, and innovative

applications. However, challenges remain, such as regulatory concerns, security vulnerabilities, and the need for scalability to support widespread adoption.

As the cryptocurrency industry evolves, governments and regulatory bodies are working to establish frameworks to govern token offerings and ensure investor protection. Additionally, the development of interoperability protocols aims to enhance the compatibility and connectivity between different blockchain networks, enabling seamless token transfers and smart contract execution.

Conclusion:
Cryptocurrency tokens and smart contracts are integral to the functionality and innovation of blockchain technology. From utility tokens to security tokens and stablecoins, different types of tokens serve diverse purposes in the digital economy. Smart contracts, on the other hand, enable automation, transparency, and efficiency in agreements and transactions.

As the cryptocurrency ecosystem continues to evolve, individuals and businesses need to understand the different types of tokens and the potential of smart contracts. By embracing this technology responsibly and addressing regulatory considerations, we can harness the transformative power of cryptocurrency tokens and smart contracts to shape a more decentralized and inclusive future.

PART III: MAJOR CRYPTOCURRENCIES

CHAPTER 9: BITCOIN: THE PIONEER OF CRYPTOCURRENCIES

Introduction:
Bitcoin, created by the pseudonymous Satoshi Nakamoto in 2009, revolutionized the world of finance and introduced the concept of decentralized digital currency. This chapter explores the origins of Bitcoin, its underlying technology, and its impact on the global economy.

The Birth of Bitcoin:
In October 2008, Satoshi Nakamoto published the Bitcoin whitepaper titled "Bitcoin: A Peer-to-Peer Electronic Cash System." The whitepaper outlined a decentralized network that enables secure, peer-to-peer transactions without the need for intermediaries. Bitcoin introduced the concept of a blockchain, a distributed ledger that records all Bitcoin transactions.

Key Features of Bitcoin:
1. Decentralization: Bitcoin operates on a decentralized network, meaning there is no central authority governing its transactions. Instead, transactions are verified and recorded by a network of nodes, making it resistant to censorship and control.

2. Cryptography: Bitcoin relies on cryptographic algorithms to secure transactions and control the creation of new Bitcoins. Public-key cryptography ensures that transactions are secure and verifiable, while proof-of-work consensus ensures the integrity of

the blockchain.

3. Limited Supply: Bitcoin has a finite supply of 21 million coins. This scarcity, combined with the increasing difficulty of mining, contributes to its value proposition as a store of value.

Real-Life Examples:
1. Bitcoin's Price Surge: In 2017, Bitcoin experienced a historic price surge, reaching an all-time high of nearly $20,000 per Bitcoin. This attracted significant attention and investment from individuals and institutions alike. However, the price subsequently experienced a significant correction, highlighting the volatility and speculative nature of cryptocurrencies.

2. Mainstream Adoption: Over the years, Bitcoin has gained mainstream acceptance as a form of payment. Major companies, such as Microsoft and Overstock, started accepting Bitcoin as a means of payment, contributing to its legitimacy and utility.

Discussion:
Bitcoin's emergence and success have sparked a wave of innovation and the development of thousands of other cryptocurrencies, collectively known as altcoins. Bitcoin's decentralized nature and limited supply have positioned it as a potential hedge against traditional financial systems, inflation, and economic instability.

However, Bitcoin has also faced challenges. Scalability remains a concern, as the network's transaction processing capacity is limited. Additionally, the environmental impact of Bitcoin mining, which requires substantial computational power, has drawn criticism due to its high energy consumption.

Conclusion:
Bitcoin's creation marked a pivotal moment in the history of cryptocurrencies. Its decentralized nature and innovative use of blockchain technology have influenced the development of numerous other cryptocurrencies and blockchain-based

applications. While Bitcoin's future remains uncertain, its impact on the global economy and the way we perceive money and transactions cannot be overlooked. As the pioneer of cryptocurrencies, Bitcoin continues to shape the trajectory of the digital economy and inspire new financial possibilities.

CHAPTER 10: ETHEREUM: THE PLATFORM FOR DECENTRALIZED APPLICATIONS

Introduction:
In the world of cryptocurrencies, Ethereum stands out as a platform that goes beyond digital currency and enables the development of decentralized applications (DApps). This chapter explores the origins of Ethereum, its key features, and its impact on the blockchain ecosystem.

The Birth of Ethereum:
In late 2013, Vitalik Buterin proposed the idea of Ethereum, an open source blockchain platform that would allow developers to build and deploy smart contracts and DApps. Ethereum was officially launched in July 2015, following a successful crowdsale that raised funds to support its development.

Key Features of Ethereum:
1. Smart Contracts: Ethereum introduced the concept of smart contracts, self-executing contracts with the terms of the agreement directly written into code. Smart contracts enable the automation and execution of transactions and agreements without intermediaries, providing transparency, security, and

efficiency.

2. Ethereum Virtual Machine (EVM): The EVM is a decentralized, Turing-complete virtual machine that executes smart contracts on the Ethereum network. It allows developers to write code in various programming languages, making it accessible to a wide range of developers.

3. Ether (ETH): Ether is the native cryptocurrency of the Ethereum network and serves as a means of compensation for participants who perform computations and secure the network. Ether is also used to pay transaction fees and execute smart contracts.

Real-Life Examples:
1. Decentralized Finance (DeFi): Ethereum's programmable nature has fuelled the growth of decentralized finance applications. DeFi protocols enable users to engage in lending, borrowing, and trading financial instruments directly on the blockchain without relying on intermediaries. Examples of popular DeFi projects include Compound, Uniswap, and Aave.

2. Non-Fungible Tokens (NFTs): Ethereum's support for smart contracts has paved the way for the emergence of non-fungible tokens (NFTs). NFTs represent unique digital assets, such as art, collectables, and virtual real estate. Notable examples include CryptoKitties, which gained popularity for its unique and tradable digital cats, and the Beeple artwork that sold for a record-breaking price at auction.

Discussion:
Ethereum has played a significant role in expanding the possibilities of blockchain technology beyond cryptocurrency. Its programmable nature and smart contract capabilities have opened doors for developers to create decentralized applications that are secure, transparent, and resistant to censorship.

However, Ethereum faces challenges, particularly in terms of scalability and transaction costs. The network's limited capacity has led to congestion and high gas fees during peak usage periods. To address these issues, Ethereum is undergoing a major upgrade called Ethereum 2.0, which aims to improve scalability and energy efficiency.

Conclusion:
Ethereum has emerged as a ground-breaking platform that enables the development of decentralized applications and the tokenization of digital assets. Its programmability and support for smart contracts have revolutionized industries such as finance, gaming, and art. As Ethereum continues to evolve and address scalability issues, it is expected to play a pivotal role in shaping the future of blockchain technology and the broader digital economy.

CHAPTER 11: RIPPLE: TRANSFORMING CROSS-BORDER PAYMENTS

Introduction:
In the realm of cryptocurrencies, Ripple has made significant strides in revolutionizing cross-border payments. This chapter delves into the origins of Ripple, its innovative technology, and its impact on the global financial landscape.

The Birth of Ripple:
Ripple, initially released in 2012, aimed to address the inefficiencies and high costs associated with traditional cross-border payments. Developed by Chris Larsen and Jed McCaleb, Ripple introduced a digital payment protocol that enables fast, low-cost, and secure transactions.

Key Features of Ripple:
1. Consensus Algorithm: Ripple employs a unique consensus algorithm called the XRP Ledger Consensus Protocol (formerly known as the Ripple Protocol Consensus Algorithm). It allows for fast transaction settlement and consensus among network participants without the need for a centralized authority.

2. XRP Cryptocurrency: XRP serves as the native cryptocurrency of the Ripple network. It acts as a bridge currency, facilitating the

seamless transfer of value between different fiat currencies. XRP can be used as a liquidity tool to minimize the costs and time required for cross-border transactions.

3. RippleNet: RippleNet is a network of financial institutions, payment service providers, and banks that leverage Ripple's technology for efficient cross-border payments. It provides participants with access to a standardized infrastructure and rules for seamless transaction settlement.

Real-Life Examples:
1. Santander One Pay FX: Santander, one of the largest banks globally, utilizes Ripple's technology for its cross-border payment platform called One Pay FX. The platform allows customers to send and receive international payments quickly and securely using Ripple's blockchain technology.

2. MoneyGram Partnership: Ripple has formed a strategic partnership with MoneyGram, a global money transfer company, to explore the benefits of using Ripple's technology in the remittance market. The partnership aims to improve the speed and cost-effectiveness of cross-border transfers.

Discussion:
Ripple's technology has the potential to revolutionize cross-border payments by reducing transaction costs, minimizing settlement times, and enhancing transparency. Its ability to facilitate frictionless transfers between different currencies has garnered significant interest from financial institutions worldwide.

However, Ripple has faced regulatory challenges, particularly regarding the classification of XRP as a security. This has impacted Ripple's partnerships and led to legal disputes. As the regulatory landscape evolves, the outcome of these challenges will shape Ripple's future and its ability to further transform cross-border payments.

Conclusion:

Ripple has made substantial strides in transforming the traditional cross-border payments landscape. Its innovative technology, powered by the XRP Ledger Consensus Protocol, enables fast, secure, and cost-effective transactions. Through partnerships with major financial institutions and the development of RippleNet, Ripple is making significant progress in reshaping the way money moves globally.

As regulatory frameworks adapt to the growing influence of cryptocurrencies, Ripple's ability to navigate these challenges will determine its long-term success. Nonetheless, its impact on cross-border payments has already demonstrated the potential for blockchain technology to revolutionize the global financial system, providing faster, more affordable, and more inclusive financial services to individuals and businesses worldwide.

CHAPTER 12: LITECOIN, BITCOIN CASH, AND OTHER ALTCOINS

Introduction:
In the vast landscape of cryptocurrencies, Bitcoin may be the most well-known, but it is not alone. This chapter explores alternative cryptocurrencies, commonly known as altcoins, with a specific focus on Litecoin and Bitcoin Cash. We will delve into their unique features, differences from Bitcoin, and their impact on the cryptocurrency ecosystem.

Understanding Altcoins:
Altcoins refer to any digital currencies that are alternatives to Bitcoin. While Bitcoin pioneered the concept of cryptocurrencies, altcoins emerged to address various aspects such as scalability, transaction speed, and privacy. These alternative cryptocurrencies seek to offer different functionalities and improve upon certain limitations of Bitcoin.

Litecoin: The Silver to Bitcoin's Gold:
Litecoin, launched in 2011 by Charlie Lee, positions itself as the "silver" to Bitcoin's "gold." It shares many similarities with Bitcoin but aims to provide faster transaction confirmation times and a different hashing algorithm known as Scrypt. This algorithm allows for increased mining efficiency and wider accessibility for

individual miners.

Bitcoin Cash: Forking the Path:
Bitcoin Cash emerged because of a hard fork in the Bitcoin blockchain in 2017. The fork was driven by disagreements within the Bitcoin community regarding the scalability and transaction speed of Bitcoin. Bitcoin Cash sought to increase the block size limit to accommodate more transactions and enhance scalability, aiming to become a more efficient medium of exchange.

Other Altcoins:
Apart from Litecoin and Bitcoin Cash, the cryptocurrency market is home to numerous altcoins, each with its unique features and objectives. Some notable altcoins include Ethereum, Ripple, Cardano, and Binance Coin. These altcoins offer various functionalities, such as smart contract capabilities, faster transaction confirmation, or specific use cases within decentralized applications.

Real-Life Examples:
1. Litecoin: Over the years, Litecoin has gained widespread adoption and merchant acceptance due to its faster block confirmation time compared to Bitcoin. It has become a popular cryptocurrency for everyday transactions and has also been integrated into payment processors and online platforms.

2. Bitcoin Cash: Bitcoin Cash's larger block size has enabled it to handle more transactions, making it attractive for merchants and individuals who require fast and scalable payments. Some notable platforms that accept Bitcoin Cash include BitPay, a global cryptocurrency payment service provider, and e-commerce websites like Overstock.com.

Discussion:
The emergence of altcoins highlights the dynamism and innovation within the cryptocurrency ecosystem. While Bitcoin remains the dominant force, altcoins provide alternatives that address specific needs and offer diverse functionalities. However,

the proliferation of altcoins also raises concerns about market fragmentation and the potential for confusion among users.

Investors and enthusiasts should carefully evaluate altcoins, considering factors such as the team behind the project, technological innovations, adoption rate, and overall market sentiment. It is important to note that the cryptocurrency market is highly volatile, and investments should be made with thorough research and a clear understanding of the associated risks.

Conclusion:
Litecoin, Bitcoin Cash, and other altcoins have made significant contributions to the development and diversification of the cryptocurrency ecosystem. Each altcoin offers unique features, addressing specific limitations of Bitcoin and aiming to provide alternative solutions for various use cases.

While Bitcoin remains the most well-known and widely adopted cryptocurrency, altcoins continue to drive innovation and offer new possibilities for decentralized finance, smart contracts, and other applications. Understanding the different features and purposes of altcoins allows individuals and businesses to make informed decisions when engaging with the vast world of cryptocurrencies, contributing to the ongoing evolution of the brave new economy.

PART IV: CRYPTOCURRENCY USE CASES AND APPLICATIONS

CHAPTER 13: CRYPTOCURRENCIES IN ONLINE PAYMENTS AND E-COMMERCE

Introduction:
In an increasingly digital world, cryptocurrencies have gained prominence as a viable alternative to traditional payment methods in online transactions. This chapter explores the role of cryptocurrencies in online payments and e-commerce, highlighting their benefits, challenges, and real-life examples of their integration into the digital economy.

The Rise of Cryptocurrencies in Online Payments:
Cryptocurrencies offer several advantages for online payments, including decentralization, security, lower transaction fees, and faster cross-border transactions. As a result, more businesses and individuals are embracing cryptocurrencies as a means of conducting online transactions, both for purchasing goods and services and for accepting payments.

Cryptocurrencies as a Payment Option:
Numerous online merchants and service providers have started accepting cryptocurrencies as a payment option. Companies such as Microsoft, Expedia, and Overstock.com have integrated cryptocurrencies into their payment systems, allowing customers to purchase products and services using Bitcoin, Litecoin, or other

supported cryptocurrencies.

Real-Life Examples:
1. Expedia: The online travel giant Expedia started accepting Bitcoin as a payment option in 2014. Customers can use Bitcoin to book hotels, flights, and other travel-related services. Expedia's move showcased the growing acceptance of cryptocurrencies in the travel industry.

2. Shopify: As a leading e-commerce platform, Shopify allows merchants to accept cryptocurrencies through third-party payment gateways. This integration enables online businesses to cater to a broader customer base and provide seamless cryptocurrency payment options.

Challenges and Considerations:
While cryptocurrencies offer benefits in online payments, several challenges must be addressed for wider adoption. These challenges include price volatility, regulatory uncertainty, scalability issues, and user experience hurdles. Overcoming these challenges is crucial for cryptocurrencies to become a mainstream payment method.

The Role of Stablecoins:
Stablecoins, which are cryptocurrencies pegged to stable assets like fiat currencies, aim to address the price volatility associated with other cryptocurrencies. Stablecoins provide stability and a reliable medium of exchange for online payments, making them attractive for e-commerce transactions.

Cryptocurrency Payment Processors:
To facilitate the acceptance of cryptocurrencies in online payments, payment processors play a crucial role. Companies like BitPay and CoinGate provide merchants with payment processing services, converting cryptocurrencies into fiat currencies or stablecoins, reducing the volatility risk for merchants.

Security and Fraud Prevention:

Cryptocurrencies offer enhanced security measures compared to traditional payment methods. The use of cryptographic technology ensures secure transactions, reducing the risk of fraud and chargebacks. Additionally, the transparency and immutability of blockchain technology provide an auditable and tamper-proof record of transactions.

Conclusion:
Cryptocurrencies are increasingly shaping the landscape of online payments and e-commerce. Their advantages, such as decentralization, security, and cost-effectiveness, make them an attractive option for businesses and consumers alike. Real-life examples of companies integrating cryptocurrencies into their payment systems demonstrate the growing acceptance and adoption of digital currencies in online transactions.

However, challenges remain, including price volatility, scalability, and regulatory concerns. As the cryptocurrency ecosystem continues to evolve, addressing these challenges will be crucial for widespread adoption. Cryptocurrencies, alongside traditional payment methods, offer a dynamic and diversified approach to online payments, enabling individuals and businesses to participate in the ever-evolving digital economy.

CHAPTER 14: CRYPTOCURRENCIES IN REMITTANCES AND FINANCIAL INCLUSION

Introduction:
The use of cryptocurrencies in remittances and financial inclusion has gained attention as these digital assets offer potential solutions to the challenges faced by traditional remittance systems. This chapter explores how cryptocurrencies are being utilized to facilitate remittances and promote financial inclusion, examining their benefits, challenges, and real-life examples of their impact.

Cryptocurrencies in Remittances:
Remittances play a vital role in the global economy, with millions of people relying on these cross-border money transfers to support their families and communities. Cryptocurrencies present an alternative solution to traditional remittance systems by offering lower costs, faster transactions, and increased accessibility.

Benefits of Cryptocurrencies in Remittances:
1. Lower Costs: Traditional remittance services often involve high fees and unfavourable exchange rates. Cryptocurrencies can significantly reduce these costs, as they eliminate intermediaries and minimize transaction fees.

2. Faster Transactions: Cryptocurrencies facilitate near-instantaneous transactions across borders, bypassing the time-consuming processes associated with traditional remittance systems.

3. Financial Inclusion: Cryptocurrencies have the potential to bring financial services to the unbanked and underbanked populations, providing them with access to a global financial network.

Real-Life Examples:
1. Stellar: Stellar is a blockchain platform designed to facilitate low-cost cross-border payments and remittances. It enables individuals and financial institutions to send and receive money in various currencies quickly and at a fraction of the cost of traditional remittance methods.

2. Ripple: Ripple's payment protocol and digital currency, XRP, aim to enable fast and affordable cross-border transactions. Ripple's network has partnered with numerous financial institutions worldwide, streamlining their remittance processes and reducing costs.

Challenges and Considerations:
Despite the potential benefits, cryptocurrencies face several challenges when it comes to remittances and financial inclusion:

1. Regulatory Frameworks: The regulatory environment surrounding cryptocurrencies varies across countries, posing challenges to their widespread adoption in remittance services. Clear and consistent regulations are necessary to ensure consumer protection and prevent illicit activities.

2. Volatility: Cryptocurrencies are known for their price volatility, which can affect the value of remittances. To address this, stablecoins pegged to fiat currencies aim to provide a stable medium of exchange for remittances.

3. Infrastructure and Awareness: Widespread adoption of cryptocurrencies in remittances requires robust infrastructure and education to ensure individuals and businesses understand how to use and secure these digital assets effectively.

Promoting Financial Inclusion:
Cryptocurrencies have the potential to promote financial inclusion by providing individuals without access to traditional banking services with secure and affordable financial solutions. Mobile-based cryptocurrency wallets and applications can enable people to store, send, and receive money, bypassing the need for a traditional bank account.

Conclusion:
Cryptocurrencies offer transformative possibilities in the realm of remittances and financial inclusion. Their ability to lower costs, increase transaction speed, and promote accessibility makes them an attractive alternative to traditional remittance systems. Real-life examples of blockchain platforms like Stellar and Ripple demonstrate the impact cryptocurrencies can have in facilitating cross-border payments and fostering financial inclusion.

However, challenges such as regulatory frameworks, price volatility, and infrastructure gaps must be addressed for cryptocurrencies to reach their full potential in remittances. Collaborative efforts between governments, financial institutions, and technology providers are essential to create an enabling environment that maximizes the benefits of cryptocurrencies while safeguarding consumer interests. By leveraging the advantages of cryptocurrencies and overcoming the challenges, we can pave the way for a more inclusive and efficient global financial system.

CHAPTER 15: CRYPTOCURRENCIES IN THE GAMING AND ENTERTAINMENT INDUSTRY

Introduction:
The gaming and entertainment industry has experienced a significant transformation with the integration of cryptocurrencies. This chapter delves into the role of cryptocurrencies in revolutionizing the gaming and entertainment landscape. It explores the benefits, real-life examples, and potential outcomes of incorporating cryptocurrencies into these industries.

Cryptocurrencies in Gaming:
Cryptocurrencies have seamlessly integrated into the gaming industry, offering a range of benefits for players and developers alike. They enable secure and transparent transactions, decentralized ownership of in-game assets, and innovative monetization models.

Benefits of Cryptocurrencies in Gaming:
1. Secure Transactions: Cryptocurrencies provide a secure method of conducting transactions within games, protecting players' financial information, and reducing the risk of fraud or data

breaches.

2. Decentralized Ownership: Through blockchain technology, cryptocurrencies empower players with true ownership of in-game assets. These assets can be bought, sold, and traded outside the gaming ecosystem, creating a new and robust marketplace for virtual goods.

3. Enhanced Monetization Models: Cryptocurrencies have introduced novel monetization models such as microtransactions, in-game rewards, and tokenized economies. Players can earn and spend cryptocurrencies within the game environment, increasing their engagement and providing developers with new revenue streams.

Real-Life Examples:
1. Enjin: Enjin is a blockchain platform that facilitates the creation and management of blockchain-based assets for games. It allows developers to integrate cryptocurrencies into their games, enabling players to own and trade unique in-game items.

2. Axie Infinity: Axie Infinity is a blockchain-based game that combines elements of trading card games and virtual pet breeding. Players can earn cryptocurrency (Axie Infinity Shards or AXS) by playing the game and selling their in-game assets on decentralized marketplaces.

Impact on the Gaming Industry:
1. Play-to-Earn Concept: Cryptocurrencies have given rise to the "play-to-earn" concept, where players can earn tangible value by actively participating in games. This has the potential to empower players in regions with limited economic opportunities, providing a means of income through gaming.

2. Non-Fungible Tokens (NFTs) and Virtual Assets: The introduction of non-fungible tokens has gained momentum in the gaming industry. NFTs allow for the creation and trading of unique virtual assets, providing players with a sense of true

ownership and enabling developers to monetize their creations.

Challenges and Considerations:
1. Scalability: The scalability of blockchain networks is a critical challenge when integrating cryptocurrencies into games, as high transaction volumes can lead to network congestion and slower processing times.

2. Regulatory Landscape: The regulatory environment surrounding cryptocurrencies in the gaming industry is still evolving. Regulatory frameworks and guidelines need to be established to ensure compliance and protect user interests.

3. User Adoption: To achieve mainstream adoption, user-friendly interfaces and educational initiatives are necessary to familiarize players with blockchain technology and streamline the integration of cryptocurrencies into gaming platforms.

Conclusion:
Cryptocurrencies have brought about a transformative wave in the gaming and entertainment industry, introducing new possibilities for players, developers, and content creators. The benefits of secure transactions, decentralized ownership, and innovative monetization models are reshaping the gaming experience. Real-life examples such as Enjin and Axie Infinity demonstrate the potential impact of cryptocurrencies in gaming.

However, challenges such as scalability and regulatory considerations need to be addressed for widespread adoption. Collaboration between game developers, blockchain experts, and regulatory bodies is crucial to unlocking the full potential of cryptocurrencies in the gaming and entertainment sector. By harnessing the benefits of cryptocurrencies and overcoming these challenges, the industry can create a more immersive, transparent, and rewarding experience for all stakeholders involved.

CHAPTER 16: CRYPTOCURRENCIES IN SUPPLY CHAIN AND LOGISTICS

Introduction:
Cryptocurrencies have emerged as a disruptive force in the supply chain and logistics industry, revolutionizing traditional systems of payment, tracking, and transparency. This chapter explores the application of cryptocurrencies in supply chain management and logistics, highlighting their benefits, real-life examples, and potential outcomes.

The Benefits of Cryptocurrencies in Supply Chain and Logistics:
1. Enhanced Traceability and Transparency: Cryptocurrencies, enabled by blockchain technology, provide a transparent and immutable record of transactions and movements within the supply chain. This enhances traceability, allowing stakeholders to track the origin, location, and condition of goods at every stage.

2. Secure and Efficient Payments: Cryptocurrencies offer a secure, decentralized method of payment, eliminating the need for intermediaries and reducing transaction costs. Smart contracts can be utilized to automate payment processes and ensure timely settlements.

3. Counterfeit Prevention: Cryptocurrencies can be used to create

unique digital certificates or tokens that represent physical assets. These digital certificates can help prevent counterfeit products by verifying the authenticity and provenance of goods.

Real-Life Examples:
1. VeChain: VeChain is a blockchain platform that focuses on supply chain management and traceability. It uses blockchain technology and IoT devices to track and verify products throughout the supply chain. In collaboration with Walmart China, VeChain has been used to track the provenance of fresh produce, enhancing transparency, and reducing food fraud.

2. Maersk and IBM's TradeLens: TradeLens is a blockchain-based platform developed by Maersk and IBM, designed to streamline, and digitize global trade. It provides a secure, tamper-proof record of transactions, documents, and shipping data, improving transparency, and reducing paperwork.

Impact on the Supply Chain and Logistics Industry:
1. Efficiency and Cost Reduction: Cryptocurrencies streamline payment processes, eliminating intermediaries and reducing transaction costs. This improves the efficiency of financial transactions in the supply chain, enabling faster settlements and reducing administrative burdens.

2. Improved Trust and Security: Blockchain-based cryptocurrencies enhance trust and security by providing a transparent and tamper-proof record of transactions. This helps to prevent fraud, counterfeiting, and unauthorized modifications within the supply chain.

3. Supply Chain Optimization: Cryptocurrencies enable stakeholders to gather and analyse real-time data on the movement and condition of goods. This allows for better inventory management, demand forecasting, and overall supply chain optimization.

Challenges and Considerations:

1. Adoption and Integration: Widespread adoption of cryptocurrencies in the supply chain and logistics industry requires collaboration among various stakeholders, including manufacturers, suppliers, logistics providers, and regulators. Integrating cryptocurrencies into existing systems and processes can be a complex task.

2. Scalability: As the volume of transactions within the supply chain increases, scalability becomes a challenge for blockchain networks. Ensuring that the technology can handle large-scale operations is crucial for its successful implementation.

3. Regulatory Frameworks: The use of cryptocurrencies in supply chain and logistics may raise regulatory concerns, particularly related to financial transactions, data privacy, and cross-border trade. Clear regulatory frameworks need to be established to address these issues and provide a conducive environment for innovation.

Conclusion:
Cryptocurrencies have the potential to transform the supply chain and logistics industry by enhancing traceability, improving payment systems, and strengthening trust and security. Real-life examples like VeChain and Maersk's TradeLens demonstrate the successful implementation of cryptocurrencies in supply chain management.

However, challenges such as adoption, scalability, and regulatory considerations must be overcome for widespread adoption. Collaboration among industry stakeholders, technological advancements, and regulatory frameworks will pave the way for the successful integration of cryptocurrencies into supply chain and logistics, leading to increased efficiency, transparency, and trust in global trade.

PART V: CRYPTOCURRENCY REGULATION AND SECURITY

CHAPTER 17:
GOVERNMENT
REGULATIONS AND
POLICY FRAMEWORKS

Introduction:
Government regulations and policy frameworks play a crucial role in shaping the landscape of cryptocurrencies. This chapter explores the various regulations and policies implemented by governments around the world in response to the rise of cryptocurrencies. It discusses the reasons behind the need for regulations, the challenges governments face, and real-life examples of regulatory approaches.

The Need for Regulations:
1. Consumer Protection: Cryptocurrencies pose risks to consumers, including scams, fraud, and hacking. Regulations aim to protect consumers by establishing standards for security, transparency, and disclosure of risks associated with cryptocurrency transactions.

2. Financial Stability: The volatile nature of cryptocurrencies can impact financial stability. Regulations are designed to mitigate risks such as market manipulation, money laundering, and terrorist financing, ensuring the integrity of the financial system.

3. Legal and Regulatory Compliance: Governments require

cryptocurrencies to comply with existing laws and regulations, such as anti-money laundering (AML) and know-your-customer (KYC) requirements. Regulations aim to prevent illegal activities and ensure compliance with tax laws.

Real-Life Examples:
1. United States: The U.S. Securities and Exchange Commission (SEC) has taken a proactive approach to regulating cryptocurrencies. It has classified certain cryptocurrencies as securities and imposed registration and reporting requirements on cryptocurrency offerings. Additionally, the Financial Crimes Enforcement Network (FinCEN) enforces AML and KYC regulations for cryptocurrency businesses.

2. European Union: The EU has introduced the Fifth Anti-Money Laundering Directive (AMLD5), which includes cryptocurrencies in its regulatory framework. It requires cryptocurrency exchanges and wallet providers to conduct customer due diligence and report suspicious activities.

Discussion on Regulatory Approaches:
1. Prohibition: Some countries, like China, have adopted a stringent approach by banning cryptocurrency-related activities. However, complete prohibition raises concerns about stifling innovation and driving cryptocurrency activities underground.

2. Legal Frameworks: Other countries, such as Japan and Switzerland, have embraced cryptocurrencies by creating legal frameworks that define cryptocurrencies and establish rules for their operation. This approach aims to provide clarity and promote innovation while addressing regulatory concerns.

3. Sandbox Approaches: Regulatory sandboxes, as seen in the United Kingdom and Singapore, allow cryptocurrency start-ups to operate within a controlled environment, testing their business models while adhering to specific regulatory requirements. This approach balances innovation and risk management.

Challenges and Considerations:
1. Global Coordination: Cryptocurrencies operate across borders, making global coordination among governments essential. Harmonizing regulations can help prevent regulatory arbitrage and ensure consistent rules for market participants.

2. Technological Advancements: Cryptocurrencies and their underlying technologies are evolving rapidly, posing challenges for regulators to keep pace with emerging trends. Governments need to develop flexible regulations that accommodate technological advancements.

3. Balancing Innovation and Risk: Governments face the challenge of striking a balance between fostering innovation and managing the risks associated with cryptocurrencies. Overly restrictive regulations may impede innovation, while lax regulations can lead to increased risks for consumers and the financial system.

Conclusion:
Government regulations and policy frameworks are essential for the responsible and sustainable development of cryptocurrencies. Real-life examples such as the regulatory approaches in the United States and the European Union highlight the different approaches taken by governments to address the challenges posed by cryptocurrencies.

Balancing consumer protection, financial stability, and legal compliance is crucial in creating a conducive environment for cryptocurrencies to thrive. Global coordination, technological adaptability, and a balanced approach to innovation and risk management are key factors that governments must consider when formulating effective regulations. By striking the right balance, governments can foster the growth of cryptocurrencies while protecting consumers and maintaining the integrity of the financial system.

CHAPTER 18:
SECURITY RISKS AND
BEST PRACTICES IN
CRYPTOCURRENCY

Introduction:
In the world of cryptocurrencies, security is of paramount importance. This chapter explores the various security risks associated with cryptocurrencies and provides best practices to mitigate these risks. It discusses the vulnerabilities in cryptocurrency systems, the implications of security breaches, and real-life examples of security incidents.

Understanding Security Risks:
1. Phishing and Social Engineering: Hackers employ phishing techniques to trick users into revealing their sensitive information, such as private keys or login credentials. Social engineering tactics manipulate individuals into making security mistakes.

2. Malware and Ransomware: Malicious software can compromise cryptocurrency wallets and steal private keys. Ransomware attacks encrypt users' data and demand ransom payments in cryptocurrencies.

3. Exchange Hacks: Cryptocurrency exchanges are attractive targets for hackers due to the large amounts of digital assets

stored on their platforms. Successful breaches can result in significant financial losses for individuals and businesses.

4. Ponzi Schemes and Scams: Fraudulent schemes and scams in the cryptocurrency space deceive users into investing in fake projects or Ponzi schemes, leading to financial losses.

Best Practices for Cryptocurrency Security:
1. Secure Wallet Management: Use hardware wallets or cold storage solutions to store cryptocurrencies offline. Implement strong passwords and enable two-factor authentication for wallet access.

2. Regular Software Updates: Keep wallets, operating systems, and other cryptocurrency-related software up to date with the latest security patches to protect against known vulnerabilities.

3. Phishing Awareness: Be cautious of phishing attempts and never click on suspicious links or provide personal information to unknown sources. Verify the authenticity of websites and communication channels.

4. Backup and Recovery: Regularly back up wallet data and private keys, storing them securely in multiple locations. This ensures the ability to recover funds in the event of device loss or failure.

5. Secure Network Practices: Use secure and private networks when accessing cryptocurrency-related platforms. Avoid using public Wi-Fi networks, which may be vulnerable to eavesdropping and data interception.

Real-Life Examples:
1. Mt. Gox Hack: The Mt. Gox exchange, once the largest Bitcoin exchange, suffered a massive security breach in 2014, resulting in the loss of approximately 850,000 bitcoins. The incident highlighted the vulnerability of centralized exchanges and the importance of secure storage practices.

2. Parity Wallet Breach: In 2017, a vulnerability in the Parity

multisig wallet smart contract led to the loss of millions of dollars' worth of Ethereum. The incident underscored the need for thorough auditing and testing of smart contracts.

Discussion on Security Measures:

1. Multi-Factor Authentication: Implementing additional layers of authentication, such as biometrics or hardware tokens, strengthens security by requiring multiple forms of verification.

2. Cryptographic Security: Strong encryption and cryptographic protocols ensure the confidentiality and integrity of transactions and data.

3. Security Audits and Penetration Testing: Regular security audits and penetration testing help identify vulnerabilities and weaknesses in cryptocurrency systems, allowing for timely mitigation.

Conclusion:

Security is a critical aspect of the cryptocurrency ecosystem. Understanding the risks and implementing best practices is essential to safeguard digital assets and protect against potential security breaches. Real-life examples, such as the Mt. Gox hack and the Parity wallet breach, highlight the repercussions of inadequate security measures.

By following best practices such as secure wallet management, regular software updates, and phishing awareness, individuals and businesses can enhance the security of their cryptocurrency holdings. Additionally, industry-wide initiatives, including security audits and strong cryptographic protocols, contribute to the overall resilience of the cryptocurrency ecosystem. With a proactive approach to security, users can confidently navigate the world of cryptocurrencies while minimizing the risks associated with security breaches.

CHAPTER 19: COMBATING MONEY LAUNDERING AND FRAUD IN CRYPTOCURRENCIES

Introduction:
Cryptocurrencies have gained popularity not only among legitimate users but also among criminals seeking to exploit their features for illicit activities. This chapter delves into the challenges of money laundering and fraud in the cryptocurrency space and explores the measures taken to combat these issues. It discusses the techniques used by criminals, the regulatory landscape, and real-life examples of money laundering and fraud involving cryptocurrencies.

Understanding Money Laundering and Fraud:
1. Money Laundering: Money laundering is the process of disguising the origins of illegally obtained funds to make them appear legitimate. Cryptocurrencies provide an avenue for criminals to launder money due to their pseudonymous nature and the potential for cross-border transactions without traditional banking channels.

2. Fraudulent Schemes: Cryptocurrencies have been targeted by various fraudulent schemes, including Ponzi schemes, initial coin

offering (ICO) scams, and fake investment opportunities. These schemes deceive unsuspecting individuals into investing their funds, resulting in financial losses.

3. Darknet Marketplaces: The darknet, accessed through anonymizing networks like Tor, has facilitated the illegal trade of drugs, weapons, and other contraband using cryptocurrencies as a means of payment.

Combatting Money Laundering and Fraud:
1. Know Your Customer (KYC) and Anti-Money Laundering (AML) Regulations: Regulatory frameworks are being established worldwide to require cryptocurrency exchanges and service providers to implement KYC and AML procedures. These measures aim to identify and verify the identities of users, detect suspicious transactions, and report them to relevant authorities.

2. Blockchain Analytics and Monitoring Tools: Advanced analytics tools and blockchain forensics help trace and analyse transactions on public blockchains, aiding in the detection of suspicious activities and illicit flows of funds.

3. Collaboration Between Authorities and Exchanges: Cooperation between law enforcement agencies and cryptocurrency exchanges is crucial in combating money laundering and fraud. Exchanges play a pivotal role in reporting suspicious transactions and cooperating with investigations.

Real-Life Examples:
1. Silk Road: Silk Road was a notorious darknet marketplace that operated from 2011 to 2013. It facilitated the sale of drugs and other illegal goods using Bitcoin as the primary means of payment. The case led to the arrest and conviction of its founder, Ross Ulbricht, highlighting the role of cryptocurrencies in enabling illicit activities.

2. Bitfinex Hack: In 2016, the Bitfinex cryptocurrency exchange was hacked, resulting in the theft of approximately 120,000

bitcoins. The incident shed light on the importance of robust security measures and the need for exchanges to strengthen their defences against cyberattacks.

Discussion on Combating Money Laundering and Fraud:
1. Regulatory Challenges: The global nature of cryptocurrencies presents challenges for regulators, as different jurisdictions have varying regulations and enforcement capabilities. Collaboration between countries is necessary to create a unified approach to combating money laundering and fraud.

2. Privacy Concerns: Balancing the need for privacy with the prevention of illicit activities is a delicate task. Striking the right balance ensures that individuals' privacy rights are respected while providing sufficient transparency for law enforcement and regulatory purposes.

3. Education and Awareness: Enhancing public awareness and educating users about the risks associated with cryptocurrencies and how to identify potential scams is crucial in reducing the occurrence of fraud.

Conclusion:
Combating money laundering and fraud in the cryptocurrency space requires a multi-faceted approach involving regulatory measures, advanced analytics tools, and collaboration between authorities and exchanges. Real-life examples such as Silk Road and the Bitfinex hack underscore the need for stringent measures to protect users and maintain the integrity of the cryptocurrency ecosystem.

As the cryptocurrency landscape continues to evolve, regulators, industry participants, and users must remain vigilant and adapt to new challenges. By implementing robust regulatory frameworks, leveraging advanced technologies, and fostering awareness, the cryptocurrency community can work towards minimizing money laundering and fraud, ensuring a safer and more secure environment for legitimate users and businesses.

CHAPTER 20: TAXATION AND REPORTING OF CRYPTOCURRENCY TRANSACTIONS

Introduction:
The widespread adoption of cryptocurrencies has brought about the need for clear guidelines on how to handle taxation and reporting of cryptocurrency transactions. This chapter explores the various aspects of cryptocurrency taxation, including the determination of tax liabilities, reporting requirements, and the challenges faced by tax authorities. It provides an overview of the taxation frameworks in different countries and discusses real-life examples of taxation issues related to cryptocurrencies.

Understanding Cryptocurrency Taxation:
1. Taxable Events: Cryptocurrency taxation typically occurs when certain events take place, such as the sale or exchange of cryptocurrencies for fiat currency or other assets. Tax liabilities may also arise from mining activities, receiving cryptocurrencies as income, or earning interest on crypto holdings.

2. Capital Gains Tax: In many jurisdictions, cryptocurrencies are treated as assets subject to capital gains tax. The tax is calculated based on the difference between the purchase price and the selling

price of the cryptocurrency.

3. Income Tax: Cryptocurrency received as income, whether through employment or business activities, is subject to income tax. The value of the cryptocurrency at the time of receipt determines the taxable amount.

Reporting Requirements and Challenges:
1. Tax Documentation: Taxpayers are required to maintain accurate records of cryptocurrency transactions, including details such as the date of acquisition, sale price, and relevant exchange rates. This documentation is essential for reporting accurate tax information.

2. Exchange Reporting: Some countries require cryptocurrency exchanges to report user transactions to tax authorities, providing them with greater visibility into individuals' cryptocurrency holdings and activities.

3. International Taxation: Cryptocurrencies' decentralized nature presents challenges for tax authorities to enforce international tax laws. The cross-border nature of cryptocurrency transactions makes it difficult to track and report taxable events accurately.

Real-Life Examples:
1. IRS Cryptocurrency Guidance: In the United States, the Internal Revenue Service (IRS) issued guidance in 2014 stating that cryptocurrencies are treated as property for tax purposes. The IRS has been actively pursuing tax compliance from cryptocurrency users and has sent warning letters to taxpayers who failed to report cryptocurrency transactions.

2. Australian Taxation Office (ATO): The ATO requires cryptocurrency users to report their transactions and pay taxes accordingly. The ATO has also partnered with international tax agencies to share data and detect potential tax evasion involving cryptocurrencies.

Discussion on Cryptocurrency Taxation:

1. Lack of Standardization: The lack of global standardization in cryptocurrency taxation presents challenges for taxpayers and tax authorities. Varying interpretations and regulations across jurisdictions make it difficult for individuals and businesses to navigate the tax landscape.

2. Tax Planning and Professional Advice: Given the complexities of cryptocurrency taxation, seeking professional advice from tax experts who specialize in cryptocurrencies can help taxpayers navigate the regulations and optimize their tax positions.

3. Regulatory Updates: Cryptocurrency taxation regulations are continuously evolving as tax authorities adapt to the changing landscape. Staying informed about regulatory updates is essential to ensure compliance and avoid penalties.

Conclusion:

Taxation and reporting of cryptocurrency transactions play a crucial role in maintaining the integrity of the tax system while accommodating the unique characteristics of cryptocurrencies. Real-life examples, such as the IRS guidance in the United States and the efforts of the Australian Taxation Office, demonstrate the increasing focus of tax authorities on cryptocurrency tax compliance.

As cryptocurrencies continue to gain mainstream adoption, individuals and businesses involved in cryptocurrency transactions need to understand and comply with their tax obligations. By staying informed, keeping accurate records, and seeking professional advice, when necessary, taxpayers can navigate the complex world of cryptocurrency taxation and contribute to the sustainable growth of the cryptocurrency ecosystem.

PART VI: CRYPTOCURRENCY INVESTING AND TRADING

CHAPTER 21: STRATEGIES FOR INVESTING IN CRYPTOCURRENCIES

Introduction:
Investing in cryptocurrencies has become increasingly popular as more people recognize the potential for significant returns. However, the volatile nature of the cryptocurrency market requires careful consideration and strategic decision-making. This chapter explores various investment strategies and provides insights into key factors to consider when investing in cryptocurrencies.

1. Fundamental Analysis:
Fundamental analysis involves evaluating the intrinsic value and potential of a cryptocurrency based on factors such as its technology, development team, partnerships, market demand, and real-world applications. This strategy focuses on understanding the underlying fundamentals of a cryptocurrency before making investment decisions.

2. Technical Analysis:
Technical analysis involves analysing price charts, trading volumes, and patterns to identify trends and make predictions about future price movements. Traders who use technical analysis rely on indicators, such as moving averages and oscillators, to

guide their investment decisions.

3. Diversification:

Diversification is a risk management strategy that involves spreading investments across different cryptocurrencies to mitigate the impact of any single asset's price fluctuations. By diversifying, investors can potentially reduce the overall risk and increase the likelihood of capturing opportunities in different segments of the cryptocurrency market.

4. Dollar-Cost Averaging (DCA):

Dollar-cost averaging is a strategy in which investors regularly allocate a fixed amount of money to buy cryptocurrencies at regular intervals, regardless of the market price. This approach allows investors to accumulate assets over time and potentially reduce the impact of short-term market volatility.

5. Long-Term Holding:

Long-term holding, also known as "HODLing" in the cryptocurrency community, involves buying and holding cryptocurrencies for an extended period, regardless of short-term price fluctuations. This strategy is based on the belief that certain cryptocurrencies have long-term growth potential and can deliver substantial returns over time.

6. Risk Management:

Effective risk management is crucial in cryptocurrency investing. Investors should set clear investment goals, establish risk tolerance levels, and implement appropriate risk management strategies, such as setting stop-loss orders and regularly reviewing their portfolio allocations.

Real-Life Examples:
1. Bitcoin Investment:

Bitcoin, the first and most well-known cryptocurrency, has experienced significant price appreciation over the years. Many early investors who held onto their Bitcoin saw substantial returns on their investments. For example, those who invested in

Bitcoin during its early days and held onto it until the peak in late 2017 witnessed exponential growth in their wealth.

2. Ethereum and the Rise of DeFi:
Ethereum's smart contract capabilities have facilitated the development of decentralized finance (DeFi) applications, which offer innovative financial services without intermediaries. Investors who recognized the potential of Ethereum and invested in projects within the DeFi ecosystem during its early stages have profited from the significant growth in the DeFi sector.

Discussion:
1. Risk and Volatility: Cryptocurrencies are known for their high volatility and inherent risk. Investors must understand the risks associated with investing in cryptocurrencies and be prepared for potential market fluctuations.

2. Market Research and Due Diligence: Conducting thorough research and due diligence is essential before making any investment decisions. Investors should evaluate the technology, team, market demand, competition, and regulatory environment of the cryptocurrencies they are considering.

3. Regulatory Considerations: Cryptocurrency investments are subject to regulatory changes and potential risks associated with regulatory actions. Investors need to stay informed about the regulatory landscape and any legal developments that may impact their investments.

4. Market Sentiment: Cryptocurrency markets are influenced by market sentiment, news events, and social media trends. Investors should be aware of the impact of these factors on market dynamics and sentiment-driven price movements.

Conclusion:
Investing in cryptocurrencies requires a well-thought-out strategy and an understanding of the unique characteristics of the cryptocurrency market. By employing strategies such

as fundamental analysis, technical analysis, diversification, dollar-cost averaging, long-term holding, and effective risk management, investors can navigate the volatile cryptocurrency market and potentially capitalize on investment opportunities. However, it is crucial to conduct thorough research, stay informed, and assess personal risk tolerance before making any investment decisions.

CHAPTER 22: TECHNICAL ANALYSIS AND CHARTING IN CRYPTOCURRENCY TRADING

Introduction:
Technical analysis plays a vital role in cryptocurrency trading, helping traders make informed decisions based on historical price patterns and market trends. This chapter explores the concepts of technical analysis and charting techniques used in cryptocurrency trading.

1. Understanding Technical Analysis:
Technical analysis is the practice of analysing historical price and volume data to predict future price movements. It assumes that historical price patterns repeat themselves and can provide insights into future market behaviour.

2. Candlestick Charts:
Candlestick charts are commonly used in technical analysis to visualize price movements. Each candlestick represents a specific period and displays the opening, closing, high, and low prices. By examining candlestick patterns, traders can identify trends, reversals, and potential trading opportunities.

3. Support and Resistance Levels:
Support and resistance levels are key technical analysis concepts. Support levels represent price levels where buying pressure is expected to exceed selling pressure, causing the price to reverse or stabilize. Resistance levels, on the other hand, represent price levels where selling pressure is expected to exceed buying pressure, causing the price to reverse or face difficulty in moving higher.

4. Trend Analysis:
Trend analysis involves identifying and following the direction of price movements. Trends can be classified as upward (bullish), downward (bearish), or sideways (consolidation). Traders often use trend lines and indicators, such as moving averages, to determine the strength and duration of a trend.

5. Indicators and Oscillators:
Various technical indicators and oscillators help traders assess market conditions and generate trading signals. Commonly used indicators include Relative Strength Index (RSI), Moving Average Convergence Divergence (MACD), and Bollinger Bands. These tools provide insights into overbought or oversold conditions, trend reversals, and market momentum.

6. Fibonacci Retracement:
Fibonacci retracement is a popular tool used to identify potential support and resistance levels based on Fibonacci ratios. Traders use Fibonacci retracement levels to determine areas where price corrections or reversals may occur.

Real-Life Examples:
1. Bullish Breakout: Traders may use technical analysis to identify bullish breakout patterns, such as ascending triangles or cup and handle patterns. For example, if a cryptocurrency's price breaks above a significant resistance level with high trading volume, it may signal a potential upward trend continuation.

2. Divergence: Traders may look for divergence between the price and an oscillator indicator, such as RSI. If the price is making lower lows, but the RSI is making higher lows, it could indicate a potential trend reversal or a bullish divergence.

Discussion:

1. Limitations of Technical Analysis: It is important to acknowledge the limitations of technical analysis. Market sentiment, news events, and fundamental factors can influence price movements and may not always be reflected in technical analysis alone.

2. Combining Technical and Fundamental Analysis: Some traders incorporate both technical and fundamental analysis to gain a comprehensive understanding of market dynamics. By considering both technical indicators and fundamental factors, traders can make more informed trading decisions.

3. Timeframes and Risk Management: Traders should consider the timeframe they are trading in and align it with their risk tolerance and trading strategy. Short-term traders may focus on intraday charts, while long-term investors may analyse weekly or monthly charts for broader market trends.

4. Backtesting and Validation: Traders often back test their technical analysis strategies using historical data to assess their effectiveness. This process helps validate the reliability of the chosen indicators and identify potential strengths and weaknesses.

Conclusion:

Technical analysis and charting techniques are valuable tools for cryptocurrency traders to analyse price patterns, identify trends, and make informed trading decisions. By understanding concepts such as candlestick charts, support and resistance levels, trend analysis, indicators, and Fibonacci retracement, traders can develop effective strategies to navigate the dynamic cryptocurrency markets. However, it is essential to combine technical analysis with other forms of analysis, consider risk management strategies, and continuously adapt to market conditions for successful trading outcomes.

CHAPTER 23: RISK MANAGEMENT AND PORTFOLIO DIVERSIFICATION

Introduction:
In the volatile world of cryptocurrencies, risk management and portfolio diversification are crucial to protect investments and optimize returns. This chapter explores effective risk management strategies and the importance of portfolio diversification in the cryptocurrency market.

1. Understanding Risk in Cryptocurrency Investing:
Investing in cryptocurrencies carries inherent risks, including price volatility, regulatory uncertainties, and technological risks. Investors need to have a comprehensive understanding of these risks and develop strategies to mitigate them.

2. Risk Assessment and Tolerance:
Before entering the cryptocurrency market, investors should assess their risk tolerance. Risk tolerance is influenced by factors such as investment goals, financial situation, and time horizon. By understanding their risk tolerance, investors can make informed decisions about the amount of capital to allocate to cryptocurrencies.

3. Asset Allocation and Diversification:

Portfolio diversification involves spreading investments across different asset classes, industries, and geographical regions. Diversification helps reduce the impact of individual asset performance on the overall portfolio. In the cryptocurrency market, diversification can be achieved by investing in different cryptocurrencies, including established ones like Bitcoin and Ethereum, as well as promising altcoins.

4. Dollar-Cost Averaging:
Dollar-cost averaging is a strategy where investors regularly invest a fixed amount of money into cryptocurrencies at predetermined intervals, regardless of the market price. This approach reduces the impact of short-term price fluctuations and allows investors to accumulate assets at varying prices over time.

5. Stop-Loss Orders and Risk Management Tools:
Stop-loss orders are conditional orders that automatically sell a cryptocurrency when its price falls below a predetermined level. By implementing stop-loss orders, investors can limit potential losses and manage downside risk. Additionally, risk management tools such as trailing stop orders and take-profit orders can be used to automate risk management strategies.

6. Due Diligence and Research:
Thorough due diligence and research are essential when investing in cryptocurrencies. Investors should evaluate the fundamentals, technology, team, and market potential of the cryptocurrencies they consider adding to their portfolios. This research helps identify high-quality projects and reduces the risk of investing in fraudulent or poorly performing assets.

Real-Life Examples:
1. Bitcoin Crash of 2017-2018: The dramatic price decline in Bitcoin during the 2017-2018 bear market serves as a real-life example of the importance of risk management. Investors who had implemented risk management strategies, such as setting stop-loss orders or diversifying their portfolios, were better able

to limit their losses compared to those who did not have such measures in place.

2. Crypto Exchange Hacks: Several cryptocurrency exchanges have experienced security breaches and hacks, resulting in significant losses for investors. This highlights the importance of conducting thorough research on the security measures and reputation of exchanges before depositing funds. It also emphasizes the need to diversify holdings across multiple wallets or exchanges to mitigate the risk of a single point of failure.

Discussion:
1. Balancing Risk and Reward: Risk management involves finding the right balance between risk and potential reward. Higher-risk investments may offer higher returns, but they also come with increased volatility and potential losses. Investors should carefully assess their risk appetite and allocate their capital accordingly.

2. Regular Portfolio Review: It is crucial to regularly review and rebalance the cryptocurrency portfolio. As market conditions change, the weightings of different assets in the portfolio may shift. By periodically reassessing the portfolio's composition, investors can ensure that it aligns with their risk tolerance and investment objectives.

3. Long-Term Perspective: Investing in cryptocurrencies should be approached with a long-term perspective. Cryptocurrency markets are known for their volatility, and short-term price fluctuations can be substantial. By focusing on the long-term potential of cryptocurrencies and avoiding reactionary decision-making based on short-term price movements, investors can better weather market fluctuations.

Conclusion:
Risk management and portfolio diversification are fundamental aspects of successful cryptocurrency investing. By understanding the risks involved, conducting thorough research, diversifying

portfolios, implementing risk management tools, and maintaining a long-term perspective, investors can navigate the cryptocurrency market with greater confidence and improve their chances of achieving their investment goals. It is essential to continuously monitor and adjust risk management strategies as market conditions evolve, ensuring the preservation and growth of invested capital in the dynamic and exciting world of cryptocurrencies.

CHAPTER 24:
THE FUTURE OF CRYPTOCURRENCIES: TRENDS AND PREDICTIONS

Introduction:
As cryptocurrencies continue to gain prominence in the global financial landscape, it is crucial to explore future trends and potential developments in this rapidly evolving field. This chapter delves into the future of cryptocurrencies, examining emerging trends, and technological advancements, and making informed predictions about their trajectory.

1. Mainstream Adoption:
One of the most significant trends in the future of cryptocurrencies is the increasing mainstream adoption. As more individuals and institutions recognize the benefits of cryptocurrencies, we can expect wider acceptance and integration into everyday life. This adoption will be fuelled by advancements in user-friendly interfaces, regulatory frameworks, and improved scalability.

2. Central Bank Digital Currencies (CBDCs):
The emergence of central bank digital currencies (CBDCs) is expected to shape the future of cryptocurrencies. Several central

banks worldwide are exploring the development of their digital currencies, combining the advantages of cryptocurrencies with the stability and oversight of traditional fiat currencies. CBDCs have the potential to revolutionize payment systems, enhance financial inclusion, and drive further cryptocurrency adoption.

3. Decentralized Finance (DeFi):
DeFi is a rapidly growing sector within the cryptocurrency ecosystem that aims to recreate traditional financial instruments and services using blockchain technology. DeFi platforms offer decentralized lending, borrowing, trading, and yield farming, providing individuals with greater financial autonomy and access to a wide range of financial products. The future of cryptocurrencies is likely to see continued expansion and innovation in the DeFi space, transforming traditional financial systems.

4. Interoperability and Blockchain Integration:
As the cryptocurrency market matures, interoperability and blockchain integration are key areas of development. Projects and protocols that enable seamless communication and interaction between different blockchain networks are expected to gain traction. This interoperability will enhance scalability, and cross-chain asset transfers, and foster collaboration among various blockchain platforms.

5. Privacy-enhancing Technologies:
Privacy has been a recurring concern in the cryptocurrency space. Future developments are likely to focus on privacy-enhancing technologies, such as zero-knowledge proofs and secure multi-party computation. These advancements will provide users with increased privacy and anonymity, addressing regulatory and security concerns.

Real-Life Examples:
1. Ethereum 2.0: The ongoing development of Ethereum 2.0, a major upgrade to the Ethereum network, highlights the future

direction of cryptocurrencies. Ethereum 2.0 aims to address scalability issues by transitioning from a proof-of-work (PoW) consensus mechanism to a proof-of-stake (PoS) model. This upgrade is expected to enhance transaction speeds and reduce energy consumption, paving the way for broader adoption and increased utility.

2. China's Digital Yuan: China has made significant progress in the development of its central bank digital currency, the digital yuan. The ongoing pilot programs and trials demonstrate the potential of CBDCs to reshape the financial landscape. The digital yuan's integration into existing payment systems and its potential cross-border functionality showcase the future possibilities of state-backed digital currencies.

Discussion:
1. Regulatory Landscape: The future of cryptocurrencies will be influenced by evolving regulatory frameworks. Striking a balance between consumer protection and fostering innovation will be a crucial challenge for governments worldwide. Clear and transparent regulations can provide the necessary framework for cryptocurrency projects to thrive while addressing concerns related to security, fraud, and money laundering.

2. Technological Advancements: The future of cryptocurrencies will be driven by continuous technological advancements. Improvements in blockchain scalability, interoperability, and privacy features will contribute to their wider adoption and utility. Advancements in consensus mechanisms, such as proof-of-stake and shading, will address the scalability limitations faced by current blockchain networks.

3. Environmental Sustainability: As the environmental impact of cryptocurrency mining becomes a growing concern, the future will likely see a shift towards more sustainable mining practices. Energy-efficient consensus mechanisms, the adoption of renewable energy sources, and the development of

greener mining technologies will contribute to the long-term sustainability of cryptocurrencies.

Conclusion:
The future of cryptocurrencies holds immense potential for reshaping the global financial landscape. With increasing mainstream adoption, the development of central bank digital currencies, the expansion of decentralized finance, and advancements in interoperability and privacy, cryptocurrencies are poised to become an integral part of our everyday lives. While challenges remain, including regulatory considerations and technological scalability, the ongoing innovation, and the willingness to address these challenges will drive the future growth and maturation of the cryptocurrency ecosystem. As we look ahead, the transformative power of cryptocurrencies is expected to revolutionize financial systems, empower individuals, and foster a new era of decentralized and inclusive economies.

Conclusion:

The objective of this book, "Brave New Economy: Understanding Cryptocurrencies," has been to provide a comprehensive and informative exploration of the world of cryptocurrencies. Through its chapters, we have delved into the evolution of money, the concepts and technology behind cryptocurrencies, their advantages and disadvantages, and various real-life applications in different industries.

We began by tracing the history of money and understanding its limitations in the digital age. This led us to explore the emergence of cryptocurrencies as a decentralized and secure form of digital currency. We delved into the blockchain technology that underpins cryptocurrencies, highlighting its potential for transparency, security, and immutability.

Throughout the book, we discussed the different types of cryptocurrencies, focusing on pioneering examples such as

Bitcoin, Ethereum, Ripple, and Litecoin. We examined their unique features, use cases, and impact on various sectors, including finance, remittances, gaming, and supply chain management. Real-life examples showcased the transformative potential of cryptocurrencies, from facilitating cross-border transactions to providing financial inclusion for the unbanked.

We also addressed the challenges and risks associated with cryptocurrencies, including security vulnerabilities, regulatory concerns, and the need for responsible investment practices. Discussions on cryptocurrency wallets, exchanges, and security measures emphasized the importance of safeguarding digital assets and adopting best practices.

Furthermore, we explored the future of cryptocurrencies and identified emerging trends that are likely to shape their trajectory. This includes the mainstream adoption of cryptocurrencies, the development of central bank digital currencies (CBDCs), the expansion of decentralized finance (DeFi), and the integration of cryptocurrencies into various industries.

The conclusion of this book marks the beginning of a new era in the financial landscape. Cryptocurrencies have the potential to revolutionize the way we transact, invest, and interact with financial systems. However, as with any disruptive technology, it is crucial to proceed with caution, ensuring responsible and informed participation.

Individuals, businesses, and governments need to stay informed about the evolving cryptocurrency landscape, understand the risks and benefits, and adopt appropriate measures to navigate this brave new economy. This requires ongoing education, collaboration, and a commitment to regulatory frameworks that strike a balance between innovation and consumer protection.

As we conclude this book, it is evident that cryptocurrencies are not just a passing trend but a significant development that will continue to shape the future of the global economy. Their potential for financial empowerment, technological innovation, and inclusive participation is undeniable.

We hope that this book has provided you with a solid foundation and understanding of cryptocurrencies. May it serve as a guide on your journey into the brave new economy, where innovation, trust, and collaboration define the future of finance. Embrace the opportunities, mitigate the risks, and join the ongoing revolution in the world of cryptocurrencies.

www.ingramcontent.com/pod-product-compliance
Lightning Source LLC
Chambersburg PA
CBHW062354290526
45794CB00005B/2228